THE JOURNEY CONTINUES VOL 3

DISCOVERY OF THE FUTURE

WILLIAM HATFIELD

2

ACKNOWLEDGEMENTS

We are all on a journey through life! I want to thank all my family and friends who stand besides me and encourage me when times are tough.

I especially want to thank my aunt Viola for all her work in editing and preparing the manuscript of my first book for publishing. The knowledge she shared will help me to continue writing. Her confidence in me ignited a gift I never realized I had. God created me with many gifts and one of them is to be a writer. Thank you Jesus for your great love.

DEDICATION

I dedicate this book to the thirsty and hungry saints of God that desire an intimacy with the Holy Spirit like no other. My prayer is that you can find this journey as a source of encouragement, strength and power to overcome life's struggles and walk in a greater sense of freedom and relationship with the Holy Spirit and all within your sphere of influence.

PROLOGUE

Everybody is interested in the future. Questions are asked and internalized, meditated on and depending on the outcome of the meditation, reaction results. Our reactions are either fear based or faith based depending on the subject meditated on.

TABLE OF CONTENTS

LIFE

My Christian life has been anything but boring. The dreams, visions, prophetic utterances and the psalms that I write have been preparing me.

1 John 2:27 World English Bible (WEB)

27 As for you, the anointing which you received from him remains in you, and you don't need for anyone to teach you. But as his anointing teaches you concerning all things, and is true, and is no lie, and even as it taught you, you will remain in him.

1 John 2:27 Amplified Bible (AMP)

27 As for you, the anointing [the special gift, the preparation] which you received from Him remains

[permanently] in you, and you have no need for anyone to teach you. But just as His anointing teaches you [giving you insight through the presence of the Holy Spirit] about all things, and is true and is not a lie, and just as His anointing has taught you, [a]you must remain in Him [being rooted in Him, knit to Him].

Teach in the Strong's concordance means

Strong's Concordance
didaskó: to teach
Original Word: διδάσκω
Part of Speech: Verb
Transliteration: didaskó
Phonetic Spelling: (did-as'-ko)
Short Definition: I teach
Definition: I teach, direct, admonish.
HELPS Word-studies

1321 *didáskō* (from *daō*, "learn") – to teach (literally, "cause to *learn*"); instruct, impart knowledge (disseminate information).

In the NT, <u>1321</u> /*didáskō* ("teach") nearly always refers to teaching the Scriptures (the written Word of God). The key role of *teaching* Scripture is shown by its *great frequency* in the NT, and the variety of word-forms (cognates).

When you look at the definition of anointing you can sum it up in one sentence. "THE ANOINTING OF GOD PREPARES, TEACHES, AND DIRECTS YOU TO THE FULFILLING OF GOD'S DESTINY FOR YOUR LIFE."

Jeremiah 29:11King James Version (KJV)
11 For I know the thoughts that I think toward you, saith the LORD, thoughts of peace, and not of evil, to give you an expected end.

Jeremiah 29:11New International Version (NIV)

¹¹ For I know the plans I have for you,"
declares the LORD, "plans to prosper
you and not to harm you, plans to give
you hope and a future.

Jeremiah 29:11 World English Bible
(WEB)
¹¹ For I know the thoughts that I think
toward you, says Yahweh, thoughts of
peace, and not of evil, to give you hope
and a future.

   To have a future from God you must
first belong to God. In order to belong to
God you must be born again.

How to Be Born Again

By **Billy Graham** • *September 20, 2010*

A man named Nicodemus came to Jesus
by night. Perhaps he was afraid of
criticism or he had a desire for a private
conversation, or maybe he wanted to
know more before committing himself

to Jesus Christ. In any event, he came and asked Jesus some questions.

Jesus looked at him and said, "Nicodemus, you need to be born again" (Cf. John 3:5). In fact, He said, "Verily, verily" — and any time Jesus used that expression, He meant that what was to follow was very important. He said, "Verily, verily, I say unto thee … ye must be born again" (John 3:5, 7, KJV).

Have you been born again? Call it conversion, call it commitment, call it repentance, call it being saved, but has it happened to you? Does Christ live in your heart? Do you know it? Many people have thought a long time about religion and Christianity and yet have never made a commitment. **Are you committed to Jesus Christ?**

Nicodemus must have been stunned when Jesus said, "You must be born again." It wouldn't seem shocking if Christ had said that to Zacchaeus the tax collector or to the thief on the cross or to the woman caught in adultery. But Nicodemus was one of the great religious leaders of his time. Still, he was searching for reality.

You may go to church, but perhaps you are still searching. There is an empty place in your heart, and something inside tells you that you're not really right with God. Nicodemus fasted two days a week. He spent two hours every day in prayer. He tithed. Why did Jesus say that Nicodemus must be born again? Because He could read the heart of Nicodemus. Jesus saw that Nicodemus had covered himself with religion but had not yet found fellowship with God.

The Root of Our Problems

What causes all of our troubles in the world — lying and cheating and hate and prejudice and social inequality and war? Jesus said, "But those things which proceed out of the mouth come from the heart, and they defile a man" (Matthew 15:18). He said the problem is in our hearts; our hearts need to be changed.

Psychologists, sociologists and psychiatrists all recognize that there is something wrong with humankind. Many words in Scripture describe it. Among them is the word **transgression**: "Sin is the transgression of the law" (1 John 3:4, KJV). What law? The Law of Moses, the Ten Commandments. Have you ever broken one of those Commandments? Then you are guilty of having broken them all (James 2:10).

The word sin carries with it the idea of missing the mark, coming short of our duty, failure to do what we ought to do.

The Bible says, "All unrighteousness is sin" (1 John 5:17, KJV). And yet before we can get to heaven, we must have righteousness. God says, "Be perfect as I am perfect, holy as I am holy" (Matthew 5:48, 1 Peter 1:16).

Where are we going to get that perfection? We don't have it now, yet we can't get to heaven if we don't have it. That is why Christ died on the cross; He shed His blood and rose again to provide righteousness for us.

Another word is **iniquity**, which means to turn aside from the straight path. Isaiah said, "All we like sheep have gone astray; we have turned, every one, to his own way; and the Lord has laid on Him the iniquity of us all" (Isaiah 53:6).

The Bible says, "Therefore, just as through one man sin entered the world, and death through sin … thus death spread to all men, because all sinned" (Romans 5:12). Every person needs a **radical change**. We need to have our sins forgiven; we need to be clothed in the righteousness of God. To find fulfillment in this life we need to find something to commit ourselves to. Are you a committed person? What are you committed to? Why don't you make Christ your cause and follow Him? He will never let you down.

The New Birth

Some people ask the question: What is new birth? Nicodemus asked that question too: "How can a man be born when he is old?" He wanted to understand it.

I was born and reared on a dairy farm. How can a black cow eat green grass and produce white milk and yellow butter? I don't understand that. I might say, "Because I don't understand it, I'm never going to drink milk again." And you'd say, "You're crazy."

I don't understand it, but I accept it by faith. Nicodemus could see only the physical and the material, but Jesus was talking about the spiritual.

How is the new birth accomplished? We cannot inherit new birth. The Bible says that those who are born again "were born, not of blood, nor of the will of the flesh, nor of the will of man, but of God" (John 1:13). Our fathers and mothers may be the greatest born-again Christians in the world, but that doesn't make us born-again Christians, too. Many people have the idea that because they were born into a Christian home, they are automatically Christians. They're not.

We cannot work our way to God, either. The Bible says that salvation comes "not by works of righteousness which we have done, but according to His mercy He saved us, through the washing of regeneration and renewing of the Holy Spirit" (Titus 3:5).

Nor is reformation enough. We can say, "I am going to turn over a new leaf," or "I am going to make New Year's resolutions." But Isaiah said that in the sight of God "all our righteousness's are like filthy rags" (Isaiah 64:6).

Some of us have changed on the outside to conform to certain social standards or behavior that is expected of us in our churches, but down inside we have never been changed. That is what Jesus was talking to Nicodemus about. He said, "Nicodemus, you need changing inside," and only the Holy Spirit can do that. Being born from above is a supernatural act of God. The Holy Spirit convicts us of our sin; He disturbs us because we have sinned against God. And then the Holy Spirit regenerates us. That is when we are born again. The Holy Spirit comes to live in our hearts to help us in our daily lives. The Spirit of God gives us assurance, gives us joy, produces fruit in our lives and teaches us the Scriptures.

Some people try to imitate Christ. They think that all we have to do is try to follow Jesus and try to do the things He did, and we will get into heaven. But we can't do it. We may know the religious songs. We may even say prayers. But if we haven't been to the foot of the cross, we haven't been born again. That is the message Jesus is trying to teach us.

To be born again means that "[God] will give you a new heart and put a new spirit within you" (Ezekiel 36:26). "Old things have passed away; behold, all things have become new" (2 Corinthians

5:17). We are "partakers of the divine nature" (2 Peter 1:4); we have "passed from death into life" (John 5:24). The new birth brings about a change in our philosophy and manner of living.

The Mystery

There is a mystery to the new birth. Jesus said, "The wind blows where it wishes, and you hear the sound of it, but cannot tell where it comes from and where it goes" (John 3:8). But you can see the result. Jesus did not attempt to explain the new birth to Nicodemus; our finite minds cannot understand the infinite. We come by simple childlike faith, and we put our faith in Jesus Christ. When we do, we are born again.

Are you sure of your salvation?

It happens this way. First we have to hear the Word of God. "Faith comes by hearing, and hearing by the word of

God" (Romans 10:17). That is the first step. "It pleased God through the foolishness of the message preached to save those who believe" (1 Corinthians 1:21). It sounds foolish that words from a Bible have the power to penetrate our hearts and change our lives, but they do, because they are God's holy words.

Then there is the work of the Holy Spirit. He convicts: "And when He has come, He will convict the world of sin, and of righteousness, and of judgment" (John 16:8). He changes us. He changes our wills, our affections, our objectives for living, our disposition. He gives us a new purpose and new goals. "Old things pass away, and everything becomes new" (Cf. 2 Corinthians 5:17). Then He indwells us: "Do you not know that you are the temple of God and that the Spirit of God dwells in you?" Does God the Holy Spirit live in you?

Jesus Christ says that we must be born again. How do we become born again? By repenting of sin. That means we are willing to change our way of living. We say to God, "I'm a sinner, and I'm sorry." It's simple and childlike. Then by faith we receive Jesus Christ as our Lord and Master and Savior. We are willing to follow Him in a new life of obedience, in which the Holy Spirit helps us as we read the Bible, and pray and witness.

If there is a doubt in your mind about whether you have been born again, I hope you will settle it now, because the Bible says in 2 Corinthians 6:2, "Now is the accepted time; … [today] is the day of salvation."

WHEN RELATIONSHIPS GO SOUTH…HOPE?

I am sitting here thinking about my marriages, and the only constant in both of them is me. It is easy to point fingers when things go wrong. So many and I would have to say too many people play the victim. I have made the choice to not be or play the victim in order to get sympathy from people. I have not or ever will be an attention getter, look at me look at me.

When you get the attention of people, you may get their sympathy for supposed wrongs that you perceive have been done to you. But be warned if they find even the littlest fault in you, you will get their judgment as well. The sin nature resides in all human flesh and trusts me you don't want the sin nature to be for you or against you. Even Jesus knew this.

John 2:23-25 Amplified Bible, Classic Edition (AMPC)

23 But when He was in Jerusalem during the Passover Feast, many believed in His name [identified themselves with His party] after seeing His signs (wonders, miracles) which He was doing.

24 But Jesus [for His part] did not trust Himself to them, because He knew all [men];

25 And He did not need anyone to bear witness concerning man [needed no evidence from anyone about men], for He Himself knew what was in human nature. [He could read men's hearts.]

So rather than place blame and point

fingers I want to analyze both situations to see if I can find something no one has noticed about failed relationships.

In my first marriage of twenty years everything seemed like a normal Canadian marriage. You have your ups and downs highs and lows. The odd disagreement even a heated argument but nothing that is different from two individuals who think of self, trying to form a union of being selfless and thinking of us rather than me, me, me. Life goes on and suddenly Jan. 26 1997 a truck accident brings a normal peaceful life to a screeching halt.

Serious brain injury took me out of commission for long time. I was recovering from the brain injury when rheumatoid arthritis set in. Typical devil kick you when you are down. My family never recovered from this hardship but fell apart. I won't go into details about the other man coming in and stealing the heart of my family. I will talk about it later. I think marriages can be summed up with the parable of the sower. I know the parable of the sower applies to the word of God and the kingdom of God, but I think we can apply it to marriage as well. Let's take a look at the parable.

Matthew 13New King James Version (NKJV)

The Parable of the Sower

13 On the same day Jesus went out of the house and sat by the sea. ² And great multitudes were gathered together to Him, so that He got into a boat and sat; and the whole multitude stood on the shore.

³ Then He spoke many things to them in parables, saying: "Behold, a sower went out to sow. ⁴ and as he sowed, some *seed* fell by the wayside; and the birds came and devoured them. ⁵ Some fell on stony places, where they did not have much earth; and they immediately sprang up because they had no depth of earth. ⁶ But when the sun was up they were scorched, and because they had no root they withered away. ⁷ And some fell among thorns, and the thorns sprang up and choked them. ⁸ But others fell on good ground and yielded a crop: some a hundredfold, some sixty, some thirty. ⁹ He who has ears to hear let him hear!"

The Purpose of Parables

¹⁰ And the disciples came and said to Him, "Why do you speak to them in parables?"

¹¹ He answered and said to them, "Because it has been given to you to

know the mysteries of the kingdom of heaven, but to them it has not been given. ¹² For whoever has, to him more will be given, and he will have abundance; but whoever does not have, even what he has will be taken away from him. ¹³ Therefore I speak to them in parables, because seeing they do not see, and hearing they do not hear, nor do they understand. ¹⁴ And in them the prophecy of Isaiah is fulfilled, which says:

'Hearing you will hear and shall not understand,
and seeing you will see and not perceive;
¹⁵ for the hearts of this people have grown dull.
Their ears are hard of hearing,
and their eyes they have closed,
Lest they should see with *their* eyes and hear with *their* ears,
Lest they should understand with *their*

hearts and turn,
So that I should[a] heal them.'[b]

16 But blessed *are* your eyes for they see, and your ears for they hear; 17 for assuredly, I say to you that many prophets and righteous *men* desired to see what you see, and did not see *it,* and to hear what you hear, and did not hear *it.*

The Parable of the Sower Explained

18 "Therefore hear the parable of the sower: 19 When anyone hears the word of the kingdom, and does not understand *it,* then the wicked *one* comes and snatches away what was sown in his heart. This is he who received seed by the wayside. 20 But he who received the seed on stony places, this is he who hears the word and immediately receives it with joy; 21 yet he has no root in himself, but endures only for a while. For when tribulation or

persecution arises because of the word, immediately he stumbles. [22] Now he who received seed among the thorns is he, who hears the word, and the cares of this world and the deceitfulness of riches choke the word, and he becomes unfruitful. [23] But he who received seed on the good ground is he who hears the word and understands *it,* who indeed bears fruit and produces: some a hundredfold, some sixty, some thirty."

Marriage is like a seed, it needs to be nourished, watered and cultivated then you will get a good return. The heart of the person will determine the return on the seeds of marriage. When someone doesn't understand marriage is a life time commitment the wicked one in the disguise of another person can come and steal the seed. Just like Satan in the garden of Eden promised Eve. The original plan wasn't good enough it will be better with this new and exciting plan.

Stony ground hearts are living in a fantasy land concerning marriage. If I get married to him/her life will be great and wonderful like living in heaven. When the partner doesn't fulfill the expectations of the other person or heaven forbid actually fails then the marriage is in jeopardy. When people's fantasy bubbles are popped everything becomes about them. They feel persecuted when reality sets in and everyone is against them. Facing reality is the greatest hardship going and they are going through great tribulation. Ask the liberals about the fantasy bubble when Trump got elected.

The thorny heart is the person entering marriage with plans of grandeur and success. They may even be good honorable plans but when life sets in they have no endurance. What I find crazy about the deceitfulness of riches is when third world country citizens compare Canada to their country. For example the Philippines currency rate bounces around the 40 to one rate fluctuating a bit. In other words our poverty level is around thirty thousand dollars which is equivalent to one million two hundred thousand Filipino pesos. So everyone in Canada is rich so marry a Canadian and you will be well off. But when life and reality sets in, you make Canadian dollars you pay bills with Canadian dollars. These individuals' dreams aren't coming to pass as quickly as they want so they perceive the marriage is a big mess they want out of.

Bottom line is the heart. Your heart condition and theirs will determine the success or failure of a marriage. You can only be responsible for yourself and not the other person. The hope for a restored struggling marriage and an overcoming partnership is to develop the fruit of the spirit in your life, repent of known sin before the Lord. What people fail to see is; outward actions are a manifestation of the inward condition of the heart. As a writer I endeavour to express how I perceive things. I have listened to many people speak negative of others in failed relationships. Failed relationships cover more than just marriage. Relationships between friends, siblings, spouses, business partners, children and parents, acquaintances and any other situations where two or more humans interact with each other are all determined by the condition of the heart.

Like I said earlier I was the only constant in the relationships. The constant in my life was rheumatoid arthritis. The first marriage was the beginning of the disease and my first wife could only see hardship and fell victim to the wiles of the devil in the form of another man who desired her for himself. This man didn't care if she was married; he lusted for her and was going to take her.

2 Timothy 3:6 ⁶They are the kind who worm their way into homes and gain control over gullible **women**, who are loaded down **with** sins and are swayed by all kinds of evil desires.

This man took up residence at the

men's hostel where my wife worked. They met and soon they began chatting into the late hours of the morning. It started off innocent enough but grew into a more personal friendship. I noticed a change in my wife as she grew more and more distant from me. Eventually I noticed that this man was a habitual compulsive liar. His claims of being a hells angel biker were absolutely absurd. But my wife fell for this because she thought it was her call in life to win bikers to Jesus. But that was a cover up for what was really going on in her heart. I noticed every time we were in a ministry situation my wife would naturally gravitate towards the men. I began to notice a pattern developing. If my wife and one her friends went to talk to some acquaintances about Jesus, she would come home and tell me about her witness to the males or the husband of the group. When I asked about the females she would just shrug it off like no big deal.

I found it odd when she insisted that we move to a particular city because she ministered to a man who was really interested in Jesus. I began to look into her family relationships in the past and found some interesting things. Her step mom was an alcoholic and fought continually with her dad. The fighting just caused him to stay away from home continually, leaving her at the mercy of an alcoholic, mean, women. This situation left my wife with a void in her life. She never got the emotional stability or the protection from a father she needed growing up. This left a void in her life that subconsciously caused her to look to men to fill it. When she left me she said that I was supposed to fulfill the emotional needs in her life and since I can't she was going to find someone who would. Thus enters Satan in a man who promises her the world without the ability to give it but is a good talker.

I am not vindictive or bitter over this situation but actually have empathy for this woman. I married a woman that was damaged by unfortunate circumstances. Not having the emotional support from her father as a little girl left her wanting as a woman. Now as of this writing she is by herself and alone and he has passed to his eternal reward from a brain hemorrhage. I believed for restoration and prayed for six years and tried communicating with her but to no avail. I finally divorced her after all hope of restoration was gone. The lesson I learned from this situation is **FATHERS BE THERE FOR YOUR DAUGHTERS BOTH EMOTIONALLY AND PROTECT THEM FROM HARM.** If they get a good foundation from their fathers as a child then adult hood will be much better.

The role of the father is very important to both children daughter and son. Satan is trying to diminish the role of the father and men in today's society. You can see in today's society as more single mothers raise their children we have a generation that is handicapped. People may say not me I am fine and nothing is wrong, but there is areas that are lacking in their lives but they just can't see them. You can't default a blind person because he can't see or a deaf person who can't see. They are trying to get through life the best way they know how.

With the first wife the seed (her wedding vows before God) planted in the ground of her heart could not produce a harvest because of a lack of understanding and no emotional root system. Not only her marriage but many other relationships with people fell apart. This woman was told by many people only the Holy Spirit can fulfill your emotional needs but she could not see this.

My second wife is a unique creation, when we met we clicked immediately. We were on the same page spiritually. She began to tell me about dreams she had of me standing behind her with my arms around her but my face wasn't visible. She got my height right 5 feet 10 inches. She expressed many dreams concerning me being involved in her life and ministry together. It was easy to fall in love with her. Our first four years were very good with the odd conflict as we were trying to find us rather than me. While we were attending Canadian churches and hung around with my Canadian friend's life was great. My wife being Filipino naturally looked for people of her own culture and country. We were introduced to one Filipino church which after being involved for a couple of years proved to us that it was not compatible with our belief system. We went back to the Canadian church and life was simple and peaceful again.

After a few months my wife found another Filipino church. This was a different church from the first church and we fit right in. I was accepted as an ordained minister and was immediately given a preaching schedule. LOVED IT.

This situation seemed so right, as I believe that I have a ministry in the Philippines. I got to experience the culture the language and the people. Contacts were made and travel arrangements in place and off to the Philippines we go. One month of ministry in the Philippines was great. Sharing the gospel in many churches and bible colleges was exciting to see the acceptance by the people. After we got back to Canada from the Philippines I noticed a slight change in my wife. The pastor was trying to develop courses to instruct potential leaders in his church. He couldn't do it by himself but the work load was too intense and it was causing conflict in his marriage. He unloaded the work on other members of his leadership team and now they were bogged down with the work. A full time job to survive and a preaching schedule and now create courses that are equivalent to a first year bible college was too much for me as I had little to no communication with my wife.

I resigned from the leadership team and the intense workload and settled for a preaching schedule with my secular job. I was content but my wife became silent. We went through a couple of months of her not talking to me no matter how hard I tried to communicate with her. Eventually she began to talk and some of her friends came over and she was explaining to them how we had marriage problems but she made the move to correct our marriage issues. I am listening to this in amazement thinking you created the situation by refusing to talk and now take credit for making it better thus making yourself look like the hero in her friend's eyes. I later learned that resigning as a pastor in that church affected my wife. As a pastor's wife that gave her status in that church and I resigning took that status away so naturally she was mad. My observation was that in the Philippine culture and probably not all inclusive but maybe the human condition there was an attitude of "What's in it for me and how does it make me look?" Definitely an interesting revelation to be found dealing with cultural differences.

Marrying a person from another culture definitely is a challenge.

So time goes on and things turn back to normal. I almost forgot before we left for the Philippines my wife asked for all my personal information and even a police record check. When I asked her why she told me it was important to be able to minister and preach in the Philippines. Thinking that she knew the system better than I because she told me that she used to work in government offices when she lived in the Philippines. When we got to the Philippines she took me to a gated subdivision that still in the finishing stages of construction. She took me to a two bedroom townhouse and informed me of a surprise; the personal info I gave her wasn't for preaching but for a mortgage on this town house that we are able to pay off in ten years and would be our retirement home when we get old. While we were paying it off her daughters and their families would live in it. I had no problems with her children living in it as it was a major improvement from their rat infested one room shack they were living in. my problem (not verbalized) was why not tell me right up front what was happening? Why the deception? I just let it go thinking nothing of it.

Time keeps ticking away and May 2016 comes with a twist. My knees get so bad from the arthritis that I can't work anymore. I finally get scheduled for complete knee replacement surgery Oct. 15 2016. For some reason my wife got withdrawn and more silent only talking occasionally. I spent the winter in recovery with a silent wife. Spring came and I received hand surgery for deformed knuckles. I noticed my wife more active with church activities and sent me an obvious message that my life was not as important as church activities.

My left knee got so bad that I needed a walker to help me get around. Another knee replacement surgery took place Oct. 2 2017 and the recovery process starts. Probably, another winter where she has to help out with household expenses, she is not a happy woman. She totally stops talking to me and begins to treat me like I don't exist. I am a patient man and try to communicate with her to no avail. The straw that broke the camel's back so to say was her text in early November that I had to find money for rent because she was moving out. I had no choice but to find another place as I couldn't afford to live there by myself. I went and gave notice and paid the final months' rent. The landlord was actually her uncle and I was surprised to hear him say that she told him that I moved out and not told her. She never revealed the whole situation to him thus making me look like the bad guy and that is fine by me. I got over trying to look good in the eyes of men because it brings more trouble than it's worth. Being family I explained the situation from my point of view. He understood and wanted to be a mediator in the situation. That was admiral of him if both parties wanted to communicate and be restored but I was the only one wanting that.

Getting the last of my stuff I noticed a box of dishes she packed for me, knowing she would not talk to me, I texted her thank you and she responded hope you have a good life. Definitely a signal of no restoration. Time to cut my losses, and move on. How does this situation fit in with the parable of the sower? The condition of the heart is the issue. The wedding vows taken before God was the seed planted in the heart. But he who received the seed on stony places, this is he who hears the word and immediately receives it with joy; [21] yet he has no root in himself, but endures only for a while. For when tribulation or persecution arises because of the word, immediately he stumbles. Being unwilling to endure to see the healing process completed it was easier to leave and reject the wedding vows made before God.

I never wrote this chapter to bring blame or condemnation on any of the participants involved. I wrote this actually for myself to try to understand from a biblical point of view why relationships fail or why they last. The conclusion I came up with is the condition of the heart is the deciding factor. I wonder at times about the phrase fell out of love. Was it really love in the first place or was it lust. Human love is bankrupt because it is conditional and has a hard time enduring. This brings me back to the subtitle of this book, "discovering the future". What is the future of relationships?

DISCOVERY OF THE FUTURE
FOR RELATIONSHIPS

I believe the future of relationships from a Christian point of view is the fruit of the spirit.

Galatians 5:22-26 22But the fruit of the Spirit is love, joy, peace, forbearance, kindness, goodness, faithfulness, 23gentleness and self-control. Against such things there is no law. 24Those who belong to Christ Jesus have crucified the flesh with its passions and desires. 25Since we live by the Spirit, let us keep in step with the Spirit. 26Let us not become conceited, provoking and envying each other.

When we as Christians take time to develop the fruit of the spirit in our lives

then our hearts become good ground.
⁸ But others fell on good ground and yielded a crop: some a hundredfold, some sixty, some thirty. ⁹ He who has ears to hear let him hear!"

Our words are the seeds planted in the ground, our hearts, which determine the success of our relationships in every area of our lives. I also believe in relationships that a correlation between the vertical and the horizontal exists.

1 John 2:9-11 ⁹Anyone who claims to be in the light but hates a brother or sister is still in the darkness. ¹⁰Anyone who loves their brother and sister lives in the light, and there is nothing in them to make them stumble. ¹¹But anyone who hates a brother or sister is in the darkness and walks around in the darkness. They do not know where they are going, because the darkness has blinded them.

1 John 3:10-12 [10]This is how we know who the children of God are and who the children of the devil are: Anyone who does not do what is right is not God's child, nor is anyone who does not love their brother and sister. [11]For this is the message you heard from the beginning: We should love one another. [12]Do not be like Cain, who belonged to the evil one and murdered his brother. And why did he murder him? Because his own actions were evil and his brother's were righteous.

1 John 4:7-21 <u>God's Love and Ours</u>

7 Dear friends, let us love one another, for love comes from God. Everyone who loves has been born of God and knows God.

8 Whoever does not love does not know God, because God is love.

9 This is how God showed his love among us: He sent his one and only Son into the world that we might live through him.

10 This is love: not that we loved God, but that he loved us and sent his Son as an atoning sacrifice for our sins.

11 Dear friends, since God so loved us, we also ought to love one another.

12 No one has ever seen God; but if we love one another, God lives in us and his love is made complete in us.

13 This is how we know that we live in him and he in us: He has given us of his Spirit.

14 And we have seen and testify that the

Father has sent his Son to be the Savior of the world.

15 If anyone acknowledges that Jesus is the Son of God, God lives in them and they in God.

16 And so we know and rely on the love God has for us. God is love. Whoever lives in love lives in God, and God in them?

17 This is how love is made complete among us so that we will have confidence on the Day of Judgment: In this world we are like Jesus.

18 There is no fear in love. But perfect love drives out fear, because fear has to do with punishment. The one who fears is not made perfect in love.

19 We love because he first loved us.

20 Whoever claims to love God yet hates a brother or sister is a liar. For whoever does not love their brother and sister, whom they have seen, cannot love God, whom they have not seen.

21 And he has given us this command: Anyone who loves God must also love their brother and sister.

The future of relationships is simple first **LOVE GOD WITH ALL YOUR MIGHT HEART AND SOUL AND DEVELOP THE FRUIT OF THE SPIRIT IN YOUR LIFE AND YOU WILL BE ABLE TO LOVE OTHERS AND ESTEEM THEM OF GREAT VALUE.**

THE SECOND

GOOD MORNING; HOW ARE YOU READY FOR THE SECOND? 😁. I couldn't sleep last night and your life came to my heart and mind. I started praising God for your life. For the influence of Godliness you have released too many if not all that have come into your sphere of influence. Time as years, months, days, and hours seems to catch our attention but we overlook the second like it is not important. Watch and prepare for the second because suddenly happened in the second not the hour day week month or year. BE BLESSED AND PREPARE FOR THE SECOND.

People and situations come into our lives suddenly or in the second. Have you enough of God's influence in your life to be prepared to meet these situations head on? Is the fruit of the spirit developed enough to be a blessing to new people? Is the peace of God and authority of God developed to confront adverse situations?

Everything in our lives happens in the second. It may take years or months or weeks to develop but we face them in the second. Most people are not prepared for the second because of the swiftness it suddenly appears. We don't have to be caught unawares of the second, a good relationship with the Holy Spirit can prepare us for the suddenly of the second.

Jeremiah 33:3King James Version (KJV)
³ Call unto me, and I will answer thee, and show thee great and mighty things,

which thou knowest not.

God never wants his children in the dark. He wants to show you the suddenly of your life. Question is do you want to know in advance so you can be prepared?

OH CANADA WHERE FORTH ART THOU?

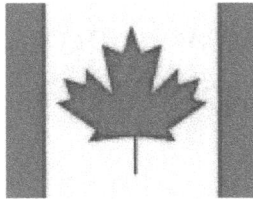

The following words, spoken on that momentous day by the Honourable Maurice Bourget, Speaker of the Senate, added further symbolic meaning to our flag:

"The flag is the symbol of the nation's unity, for it, beyond any doubt, represents all the citizens of Canada without distinction of race, language, belief or opinion."

O Canada (English version)

O Canada!
Our home and native land!
True patriot love in all thy sons
command.
With glowing hearts we see thee rise,
The True North strong and free!
From far and wide,
O Canada, we stand on guard for thee.
God keep our land glorious and free!
O Canada, we stand on guard for thee.
O Canada, we stand on guard for thee

In the light of Canada's celebration of its
150 anniversary, my friend told me that
Canada started the country on the
foundation of Christianity by Christian
forefathers, as like their belief, their God
Jesus created the world and all of us, we
are all the same before their God that's

why they treat and respect everyone the same whether you are immigrants or refugees.

So I admire their national anthem as well as their belief because they make immigrants to feel welcomed, respected and safe here.

May their God continue to bless this country that has such a big heart and care for all of their citizens who lacks nothing like heat, electricity or medical care of financial support in job loss or sickness or handicapped, as well as the immigrants and refugees.

And their people stand on guard for their country as what their national anthem said to keep this country on the right path their God has taught them. Quote from an immigrant.

CANADA the nation I live in, pray for and love. Even though Canada is not mentioned in the bible by name I believe God has a purpose and a destiny for us. I think I heard of an event of 1776 when the Americans were defeating the British they wanted to take over all of Canada because they had the military power to do so and that was part of their manifest destiny. Apparently some prophets of God stood up and declared that this was not God's plan and they should leave Canada alone. God told them that He had reserved Canada for an end time work.

Around 1776 zealous Americans sought to persecute the British Empire Loyalists who had turned north to settle in Canada in order to remain under the British rule. The

Spirit of the Lord spoke through the prophets of the Puritan Reformers saying: "Do not hinder these people, let them move to Canada. Do not seek to incorporate the land of Canada into America. I am in the independence of America from Britain, and will mightily use this country. But Canada has been reserved by Me for the last days for a special work." (Peter Marshall: The Light and The Glory)

Let's see if there are any prophetic words over Canada in the last century to give us a clue to how God is going to use our nation in the end times.

International Revival Beginning in Western Canada

From Mike & Cindy Jacobs

As shared by Mike Jacobs (husband of Cindy Jacobs), Oct 23, 2016

Mike Jacob awakened at 5 AM with the

Lord speaking and reminded him of a prophetic word that was released in the early 1980's from their prayer network:

"A REVIVAL will start in WESTERN CANADA, sweeping from the west to east, and then go down the into the United States, and into Mexico, Central America, and South America. And God was speaking to me in the morning, 'Have I not said there is going to be a REVIVAL?' So He is stirring this word once again, and we are going to start seeing this revival.

The Lord also said 'As a dynamic of this revival, there will be a significant outpouring of the Holy Spirit on Catholics - the charismatic Catholics are going to be very involved in this.' It will come like fire for the charismatic Catholic Church, and He kept saying for them 'embrace the fire!'

The Lord reminded me about a word that God gave Cindy some years ago, 'When there is this outpouring of the Holy Spirit, it will cause some of the Catholics to move away from any idolatry, the statues, and there will be like a pure branch of the Roman Catholic church, this may even cause a split to some degree in the Catholic church. The traditional evangelicals, charismatics, and Pentecostals, will be amazed at the power and the outpouring of the Holy Spirit in terms of signs, wonders, and miracles in the charismatic Catholic Church.'"

CINDY JACOBS PROPHESIES OVER CANADA -- "AN ANOINTING TO HEAL ISAAC AND ISHMAEL" --AND A WORD TO THE CHURCH ABOUT PROPHETS

Cindy Jacobs
Mar 25, 2001

CINDY JACOBS PROPHESIES OVER CANADA -- "AN ANOINTING TO HEAL ISAAC AND ISHMAEL" --AND A WORD TO THE CHURCH ABOUT PROPHETS

Sent to THE ELIJAH LIST by Pat Cocking Pat's email:cocking@telus.net Thursday, March 22, 2001

(Prophesied by Cindy Jacobs, Wednesday, March 7, 2001) Cindy Jacob's website: http://generals.org/

Psalm 72:8, 9, 12-15 He shall have dominion from sea to sea. From the river to the ends of the earth. Those who dwell in the wilderness will bow before Him and His enemies will lick the dust. And this is so powerful as you read this. He will deliver the needy when he cries, the poor also, him who has no helper. He will spare the poor and needy. **THIS IS ALL PROPHETIC FOR CANADA**.

He will save the souls of the needy. He will redeem their life from oppression and violence. And precious shall be their blood in His sight. And the verse 15, I want you to look at is - Prayer will also be made for him continually.

That's day and night. And daily He shall be praised. But the Holy Spirit is really speaking to me that there is a direct tie from here and also from Zechariah 9 where this is repeated to Daniel 7. He shall have dominion from sea to sea. You remember that we've been talking about dominion. And we've been talking about how that's not a bad word, but as an abused word it could be a bad word.

CANADA IS COMING TO A PLACE OF HER OWN ANOINTING

And the Holy Spirit just began to show me that Canada is coming to a place of her own anointing, and that there is a shift taking place even now. That's why the Holy Spirit has had you in the book of Daniel-- in verse 7:25: "He shall persecute the saints and shall intend to change times and laws." The Lord showed me clearly that during WW II when the Jews came in the S.S. Louis to the shores of Canada-- you turned away your destiny for a generation and because of that a judgment came on Canada and in that time the giants increased in the land. Abortion came in; there is no longer prayer in schools every day; bible reading, these things. How many of you as a young person had prayer and bible reading in school in Canada? OK. And so it is my understanding that in public school now they do not begin everyday with the Lord's Prayer any more that it is not that way.

AND I WANT TO GIVE YOU A WARNING

I want to say it again. Listen to me. You should pray that prayer in Psalm 73. He shall preserve you, and your children. You need to be preserved from violence. I want to tell you something if you do not overthrow this and work to put prayer in schools you will have what we have had. The shooting outside of Calgary was only the beginning of sorrows. I pray that you hear this word, because we did some intercession even about this, I believe last year or the year before. And I feel I gave you a window of grace, but you have to understand that is not enough.

EVERY SCHOOL IN CANADA NEEDS TO BE COVERED IN PRAYER

Every school in Canada needs to be covered in intercession. Every Pastor at every church in every city needs to pray and have his intercessors pray every day for the schools in their particular city. Amen? You have got to raise up watchmen on the wall. Please heed me. I want to tell you that there are no boundaries to this thing. The Bible says believe the word of the Prophets and you shall prosper. Let me tell you something. . .

Prayer needs to be made both day and night. You need to stand up. And so the Lord wants to give you dominion from sea to sea. And not only that it says in verse 26, "The court shall be seated and they shall take away His dominion to consume and destroy forever. Then the Kingdom and the dominion and the greatness of the kingdoms under the whole earth shall be given to the people, the saints of the Most High. His Kingdom is an everlasting Kingdom and all dominion shall serve and obey Him." It says He shall have dominion from sea to sea and also to the ends of the earth. It also says that in Zechariah

9. Now what does that say? I believe the Holy Spirit has shown me several things: One is that I believe that you have come to Hebron in this nation. Hebron means "alliance or union." All right? This is, I believe represented the coming of Hebron was the first place that David ruled. But he didn't have Jerusalem yet. I believe you have reached a Hebron in this nation. Between the gathering and Brian what you did.

There is a "Hebron" that has been released. All Right? And so we see that there was a rag tag band of men that became mighty in God and they became fighters. All Right? There's several things represented by Hebron. One is in Hebron that Abram's name was changed to Abraham, father of nations. Genesis 17:5. And Sarah was called mother of nations. So what are you modeling here? You have come, and I believe what you did in this past year or so, maybe you didn't know what you were doing, but God has changed the leaders in this nation from Abrams to Abraham's, from Sarai to Sarah's, and. . .

GOD IS GOING TO BREAK BARRENNESS OFF THIS NATION

God has released a fathering and a mothering anointing that is going to break barrenness off this nation and you are going to begin to see great fruit and great harvest. Amen? And you also know if you study it that-- Hebron was the place that Abraham actually purchased. And this is a sign of covenant of God. You see if you go back in the history of Canada you see there were a people that made a covenant with God for this nation. Amen? But what happened, was when you didn't go in, when you needed to go in, and take your destiny. Which was actually to heal nations and shield the Jews, and protect the Jews when they came to your shores, what happened from that time, because of what I believe was fear and many other things? We see that you didn't go on in your destiny and you can be likened to this, because Hebron was a place where the twelve spies came. And they cut the cluster of grapes in Hebron. And so Caleb came out and said [to] Joshua, "We're more than able to take this land." And so the Lord shows me that there are those who have for many years believed that this land could be taken. They were the Caleb's waiting for this time to say give me this mountain. This is your hour. The Lord also showed me this there are prayers of your forefathers and mothers that God is getting ready to answer.

JUSTICE AND RIGHTEOUSNESS RE-ESTABLISHED IN THE LAND

He is going to answer through you to re-establish justice and righteousness in this land. That there are those who have said that scripture, that He shall have dominion from sea to sea. Those who gave that to this nation as a scripture for this nation. They not only gave it but they prayed it and believed it. And there is a time when we are going to mix together the anointing of the generations.

A PROPHESIED PRIME MINISTER

And God is saying, "Do I find a generation with faith that is saying, 'let's go in and take this Promised Land.'" I believe you have come to Hebron, but it's time to go to Jerusalem. And you can see this Jerusalem in two ways. One, is that there is a physical Jerusalem, which is a governmental seat, and then you can see where Daniel 7 comes into play, that when you get the government, and the Spirit- filled prime Minister, that I have prophesied. When that happens in this nation you will have your Jerusalem. Amen? God wants to do that for you, but you're going to have to fight for it, because there are mean spirits in this land that want to stop you in Hebron. Amen? Are you getting this? So in this land it is much harder now than it would have been before. Because there's a spirit of Diversity and all these things have come in. And you know the Holy Spirit's been saying it's about your mind. Isn't it? The pluralistic thinking has to go.

LORD, WHAT DO YOU WANT SUNG, IN WORSHIP, OVER THIS LAND?

And the thinking of your forefathers and foremothers you're going to have to come to the place where we're going to say that was God's will for this nation. We don't care who says we're intolerant. We don't care what they say. We are going to the head-- the King of kings shall have dominion from sea to sea. Hallelujah. And the Lord showed me a major key to this is going to be worship. See, Caleb was a Kenesite. He wasn't of the tribe of Judah, but he came with Judah. All Right? And he got the anointing of the tribe of Judah, because he married a woman from the tribe of Judah. The tribe of Judah According to Psalm 60:7 was the law giver tribe. Judah shall be the lawgiver. All Right? So therefore you will release the law giving anointing through Judah in this land. Amen? It's not just any worship, listen to me, it's not just any worship. It's not enough to worship. You have to worship specifically. You have to get the mind of the Lord. What do you want sung over this land? What voice should be heard over the land?

What will break open the heavens? What do you want to do and do that thing! Amen? Just like you pray specifically, you must praise specifically.

THEN...YOU WILL SPLIT OPEN THE HEAVENS

Because then you will split open the heavens. Amen? So this is something God showed us as a strategy. So God knows what He is up to and He's trying to mix this anointing here in Canada. Why do you think you have Machines? Why do you think you have this incredible worship coming out of Canada?

RISE TO A NEW PLACE, ---YOU'VE COME TO HEBRON

The Lord wants you to rise to a new place. See you have come to Hebron. And now the Lord has showed me that you became fathers and mothers in the spirit and you took a hold of your destiny to go heal the nations. And that's why you are going to Israel, to Jerusalem.

TO HEAL ISAAC AND ISHMAEL

Because you have come where you are, wearing the mantle. You are going to go to Israel. Canada, I prophesy to you. You have the anointing to break open this war. I tell you there will be a war in Israel. They are saying it's going to be from Psalms 83, but I want to tell you who can bring healing for this matter. It is Canada. And you must rise up Canada! And you must go! And you must fight and you must stand. And the Lord says I have been waiting for a nation, which would have the anointing to heal Isaac and Ishmael. I have been waiting for one who will stand to begin to break apart the strategies of the enemy. And the Lord says to you Canada, Will you take it? Will you take your name as a healer of nations and go into the stronghold of the enemy and begin to establish my Jerusalem? Will you do it? Will you heal your nation?

WILL YOU PUT PRAYER BACK INTO THE SCHOOL?

Will you put prayer back in school? Will you pray for the schools of Canada? Will you send worship teams across this land? From the North to the South to the East to the West and so the Holy Spirit is showing you it's time for you to come up to a new place. I want to tell you one more thing it's better to be persecuted for righteousness sake than for stupidity. And so the Lord began to show me something.

A LIE THAT THE NEW TESTAMENT OFFICE OF PROPHET IS LESS THAN THE O.T.

He said, "Cindy, you have believed a lie." I said. "What is that Lie?" He said, "You have believed that the office of the prophet in the New Testament was a lesser gift than what I gave to the prophets in the Old Testament. So you cannot prophesy the greater things. I'm not talking about the simple gift of prophecy. The Lord said. "I don't give any lesser set of gifts. Now in the New Testament I gave the Holy Spirit. The Holy Spirit did not come ON the prophet --it was IN the prophet." The second thing was -- We have believed a lie that any prophet that prophesied erroneously should be stoned. In fact I worked that through with a theologian I want to tell you something. They were to be stoned if they led people into idolatry, or worship of false God's. Why wasn't Nathan stoned when he went to David and said, "Do whatever is in your heart", and he had to turn around and come back and say, "I made a mistake essentially"? Why wasn't Jonah stoned? Are you listening to me?

I WANT TO RELEASE A COMPANY OF PROPHETS

You're thinking about this aren't you? . . . But the Lord spoke to me and He said, "I want to release a company of prophets that will prophesy like they would in the Old Testament." The prophet knew what the king of Syria did in his bedroom. And I want to say to you, listen to me Canada.

You'll never do this if you don't step up to the plate and believe God for the greater things. God is going to hone the office of the prophet to such a degree that it will put the fear of the Lord in the hearts of the unbeliever. Listen. They're turning to tarot card readers. They're turning to those in divination, because they think they can tell them the truth. It's time for the Daniels to rise up for the courts of the king. It's time for the Daniels to be connected to the Prime ministers. Its time God wants to take us to a whole new level in the Spirit. We want to reach the higher things. And so the Lord is showing me that as you go to Jerusalem that the Lord is going to tear down ancient strongholds.

THE ORIGINAL NAME OF JERUSALEM WAS "BABYLONIAN"

The original name of Jerusalem was Babylonian and then it was Hittite, and there were fortresses that Satan had built up in Jerusalem that had never been torn down. Because they haven't had the anointing of a nation behind it.

Are you listening to me? This is not something to get in pride over; this is just something to say this is who we are as Canadians. We have this anointing. You see? And when you stand and rise up then the rest of us can rise up. And we can go in and take the land.

Amen? So the Lord says this is a new day for you. God is going to raise you up in ways that you cannot imagine. The Lord says to you I am going to send you in and you are going to have the heart of a giant killer. I am going to raise up the anointing's of David to roll the reproach of the nations I Samuel 17:26. Little David said, "isn't there any one to roll the reproach off of Israel?" The Lord says to you Canada, "I tried to connect you with the Jewish people when the S.S. Saint Louis came and your forbearers turned them away." But I would say that "there is a day to roll the reproach not only off this nation, you have begun, but you're going to pick up your mantle." And the Lord says the dominion I will give you to break the powers of division, to break the powers of brothers fighting brothers, the anointing of reconciliation, the ministry of reconciliation.

I AM EVEN NOW GETTING READY
TO RELEASE YOU TO THE ENDS OF
THE EARTH...

I am even now getting ready to release
you to the ends of the earth. The Lord
says I am getting ready to raise a nation
of reconcilers. I am getting ready to send
you to the ends of the earth. I will send
you to the difficult places.

The Lord says you Canadian leaders
will begin to be known as Norway has
been known. But they will come here
and they will sign peace agreements
says the Lord.

I'm going to use you to bring a lasting
peace. But the enemy is at your door
and the enemy wants to bring violence
in the land, the enemy wants to hurt
your land and your children to such a
degree that you will get your eyes off

the mission that I have placed before you and you will be diverted for another generation.

So the Lord says Rise up and says to the enemy enough is enough! You no longer can have my nation! I have decided to be a warrior! I have decided to stand and fight. I have decided I am going to prophesy! I'm going to evangelize.

FROM HEBRON TO JERUSALEM

I'm going to teach. I'm going to come to my place of destiny and the Lord says you will go "from Hebron to Jerusalem." And I am going to put a reigning anointing upon the head and I am going to put an apostolic anointing on the head. And the Lord says you will see my anointing go to the ends of the earth." Says the Lord.

Prophecies for Canada
Prophecy given to the Body of Christ

by George Pearson at EMIC - Wednesday, 11/01/06

The Word of the Lord for the nation of
Canada, the Great Awakening,
beginning from the West to
The East and back again, it has already
begun. It has already started. And
you're going to begin to see a
Spike, a spike at Kenneth Copeland
Ministries Canada. You're going to
begin to see a jump in the number
Of letters coming in, the number of
requests for materials for the number of
people desiring books and
Tapes…hunger, hunger, hunger,
hunger, hunger. (Tongues) The Great
Awakening in Canada is a great
Hunger. It is a great hunger for the
things of the Spirit. It is a great hunger
for the Word of God. (Tongues)
For the land has been – has been sick.
It's been ill but it's rising up, and
someone who has been ill for a

Long time and begins to rise up, the first thing they'll say is "I'm hungry. What's to eat? I'm hungry." There is
A divine hunger that is spreading across the nation. There is a divine passion that is rising up in the Body of
Christ.
Oh, Father, for that same hunger in the United States, that same passion in the United States. And
The Lord is saying to me now that what happens up north in Canada is going to rain upon the United
States. (Tongues) I see as it were something melting on a map. It's on a map and it's melting from Canada
And it's coming down into the northern parts of the country and it's beginning to bleed down through the
States, down (Tongues) down through Middle America, down through the southern part of the United
States and then reaching over into Mexico. Mexico. Mexico. Down. Down.

Down. Into Central America.
(Tongues) And the move of God that is
in South America is coming up to join it.
Oh! Oh! Oh! Oh! Oh!
(Tongues) And it will result, it will
result in a – in a move of God in the
western hemisphere, unprecedented
Because there will be renewal and
revival and revelation everywhere!
Everywhere! Everywhere!
And it's coming on down. It's coming
on down. It's coming on down. Be
prepared. Be ready for it. Get
Your team in preparation for that
because it has begun. You're going to
have to feed them because they
Are hungry.

Prophecies for Canada

**A Word from the Lord delivered by
Pastor George Pearson's at KCM
Canada's Pastors - Breakfast
Surrey BC September 15th, 2006**

A Great Awakening in Canada

Romans 13: 11-12 (NASB)
" Do this, knowing the time that it is
already the hour for you to awaken
From sleep; for now salvation is nearer
to us than when we believed. The
Night is almost gone, and the day is
near Therefore let us lay aside the
Deeds of darkness and put on the armor
of light."
There is a spiritual awakening, a Great
Awakening, coming to Canada. It will
start on the
West Coast and will travel to the East
Coast. It will then return again and will
be sustained
Throughout the Nation.
We will see an outpouring of God's
Glory in the churches. Pastors will be
receiving prophetic
Unction's that will reach out beyond
their immediate congregations. They
will receive words that will alter,

Change, transform, annihilate and create. They will, as Oral Roberts declared,

"Preach with fire in their bellies." There will be demonstrations of the Glory of God in

Churches. To the Nation of Canada, you must declare, "Wake up! Wake up! Wake up! It

Is time to get back up?"

People will be coming to Canada once again. This time, it will be different. It won't be just one church or one pastor. It will be multitudes of churches and scores of pastors.

To the Pastors and Ministers. Allow a free flow of the gifts of the Spirit in your services. Build in

Extra time for the preaching of the Word and for the demonstration of the gifts of the Spirit.

Preach the Word...

...stronger and bolder than ever before.

...without reservation or compromise.

...in the light of Jesus' impending return.

...with an end-time anointing.

Prophecies for Canada

A Word from the Lord delivered by Pastor George Pearsons at KCM Canada's Pastors - Breakfast Surrey BC September 15th, 2006 - cont'd

Operate in the gifts of the Spirit....

...refresh yourself in the gifts and their operations

...then begin to practice them.

Get my exact, precise will for your church and ministry. In order to do this, you must increase your time on

The mountain. You must spend time alone – with me – nobody else – no other voices. When you come

Down from the mountain, you will bring my message to the people. They will either submit and obey or

Rebel and leave. Don't chase them. Let them go. Even if they are "big givers", don't compromise what I give
You. You answer to me, not to man. You minister to man. But you answer to me. I am going to be putting some of you in the ministry on television
And radio. But I will only use those of you who are not interested in notoriety and fame. I will use those
Of you who are not driven by ego – with a need to be seen and recognized. I will only use the humble in
Heart in the Great Awakening – this Final Awakening before my Son returns. The politicians will be coming
To you, knocking on your doors. "Help me" they will cry. "What do we do about this issue? Give us guidance." Some of you ministers will become "speech writers." The politicians will beg you, "We need the right
Words. We need God's Word!" Changes will take place here in the political

realm. One moment, the ungodly
Will be in once, the next moment, they
will be gone, and the Godly will have
taken their place.
It's time to go up to the next level.
It's time for Canada's Great Awakening.

Prophecies for Canada

**Prophecy give to the Body of Christ by
Kenneth Copeland at the Vancouver,
Victory Campaign,
Vancouver BC, 06-07-02
The Glory is rising! This is it!**
[Tongues]… [PROPHECY] I've said it in
times past and I'll say it again, in the
Name of the Lord Jesus
Christ of Nazareth, I see it in the Spirit. I
see what the Lord has been saying, that
the power and the glory
Of God being manifest even as we stand
here tonight is moving and rising like a
tide. And it's rising and
Rising and rising, is rising up to the

place where it is now, and will continue to be more and more visible in

The natural physical world as in the days of old when they said, "We see the cloud of God on yonder hill.

We see the fire of God on yonder hill." But out of your belly shall flow Rivers of living water. And the glory

flow up and out of you! And manifestations of great glory, beyond anything the human race has ever seen

In all of its history, manifestations of the Most High God in fullness of expression is due in these days now.

And He has planned a major portion of it to take root…which it has, to take seed…which it has,

And to begin to grow…which it has, right out of the heart of the Canadian people. And will grow, and will

Grow, and will grow. At first it will be seen in different places around, but then as it grows and becomes

More and more powerful, and more and

more expressive, suddenly it will burst out even in the midst of
Strange and funny religions. It'll break out in strange places. It'll break out in churches that don't even
Believe in it. And it'll break out in places around the world, and it'll be right here among the Canadian
People and it will explode upward first, and then begin to spread out. And it'll spread out over the top of
The world and down the other side, and it'll spread out and _ow downward from here, down into the
United States, down into the Mexico's and into the Caribbean, and around this world!
And it will become known all over the world people are getting healed in Vancouver! People are
Getting healed in Toronto!
Now I kept My Word, saith the Lord, and I started this in several places among the Canadian people,

And it became known as the Toronto Blessing. Well, in the first place, it wasn't the Toronto Blessing. It was The blessing of Abraham through Jesus. But now the next wave is upon you. And it won't be in just a place Or two or a spot or two. And what happened in Toronto, and what happened in Pensacola, and what Happened in Brownsville, and what's been happening in a number of ministries for many years, people will Look at it and say, "Whooh! That was just kids' play. Man, look at this!" A great sweeping of souls has Begun throughout the earth. No wicked religion can stop it. No government can stop it. For I have determined In My way and in my time, and my way is the way, and my time is now.

Prophecies for Canada

Prophecy give to the Body of Christ by

**Kenneth Copeland at the Vancouver,
Victory Campaign,
Vancouver BC, 06-07-02 - cont'd**

This is it! This is it. This is it. I keep
hearing the Spirit of God say that. This
is it! This is it! This is

What all the prophesying has been
about. This is what your grandmother
and granddaddy prayed over.

This is it. This is it! This is it!

Oh, hallelujah!

Now some will make stupid and foolish
decisions and miss it. Some will miss a
part of it and say,

"Ooh, no, I repent," and jive back into it.
Some people through pride and
ignorance and yielding to foolish

And silly religious ideas will miss the
whole thing.

There are some religious fools who will
try to stop it. And I will deal with them
in mercy, and I will

Work with them as long as I can, but
should they continue to rebel and to

refuse my grace, then the same
Anointing that removes burdens and
destroys yokes will have to remove
them because they've become a
Burden.
Not My will, saith the Lord, it is my will
that all of you get in it and enjoy it. But
there are those that
Will foolishly resist me. And in these
last days, that is not a smart thing to do.
The best is to make the heart
adjustments and be willing and
obedient. Willing to be willing.
Willing to go. Willing to stay. Willing to
shout. Willing to pray. Hallelujah.
Willing to be still and know that
I am God, Who is love. And willing to
jump and run to the ends of the earth
and take this message that
Jesus is alive.
And those that will rise up and receive
My Voice and receive my callings and
receive my urgings to
Them, I will through them show myself

alive and together we will enjoy the wonders and the miraculous

And the manifestations of my glory that I have longed for 6,000 years to display and to lavish on you.

These are my times, saith the Lord, and they are your times, saith the Lord. So rejoice and be glad in

It, for the glory of the Lord is shining on you now. Hallelujah! Whooh! Glory, glory, glory, glory, glory,

Glory, glory! Glory, glory, glory, glory, glory, glory, glory. Hallelujah! Hallelujah, hallelujah, hallelujah, Hallelujah, hallelujah. Bless the Lord. [END OF PROPHECY]

Prophecies for Canada

Kenneth Copeland - 1996 South West Believers Convention - August 5, 1996
...and one little Holy Ghost tongue-talking, healing-believing mother can lay in the door before God

And change the whole thing.
And that's what's about to happen.
There are some changes coming in the
United States. There are
Some changes coming in Canada. There
are some changes coming in the
Philippine Islands. There are
Some changes coming in Australia, but
it's not going to be to the open degree
that it is to the United
States and Canada and to the Philippine
Islands.
There are some drastic overwhelming
changes that are about to take place in
the United States,
Canada and in the Philippine
Islands...some in Australia — that are
absolutely going to shock the nations of
The world.
And there's no use you standing there
trying to figure out what it is, because it
isn't never happened
Before! And it's exceeding abundantly
beyond what you or I can ask or think.

100

Our God is on the
Move and the changes are coming!
So just rejoice. Just rejoice and bless His
Name.

Prophecies for Canada

1995 Canada Victory Campaign - Kenneth Copeland - Thurs, Oct. 26 7:30 p.m.
The Outpouring

Oh, they've been telling me you can't
have revival there too, saith the Lord.
They've been telling me
That for years. They've been telling me
for years that people in this part of the
world don't want to hear the
Word of God.
But I'm moving, saith the Lord, and
that's being disproved every place,
every hour. But in this place,
I have picked this spot, this very spot
upon which you sit and stand this night,
I have picked this spot, saith

The Lord, to become a fountain and to become an explosive outpouring that will _ow from here out into
The rest of this nation, out into the rest of this part of the world and then roll and _ow to the south and
_ow down through the United States and all the way into Central America, to _ow to the east, to _ow to
The west, to _ow to the uttermost parts of this earth.
And people will say, "My, are you part of that group from Toronto and Hamilton? Are you part of?
That group that's come out of there?" They're already saying that, saith the Lord. But I'll tell you what, you
Think they've already begun to talk about the Toronto blessing, they're about to start talking about the Toronto explosion. Because there's coming an explosion. There's coming a blowout of the power of the
Living God. And it will _ow like a river

of molten love and glory that will _ow
like a white-hot river that will
Consume all in its path with the glory
and the peace and the anointing and the
goodness of God.
So give thanks and give praise, saith the
Lord. For there are churches right here
in this city of Hamilton
That this night forward will never be the
same again. There is a beginning here
and it will continue,
Saith the Lord. I'm not going to allow
politics to mess it up. I'm not going to
allow anything else to mess it
Up. There are people that still have the
idea that they can do whatever they
want to and that I won't have
Anything to do or to say about it, saith
the Lord, but my schedule has been
changed somewhat.
There have been times that I could allow
you more and more and more time to
repent of this and
Repent of that and all of these kinds of

things, but I am now on the End-Time clock. I have moved on to a

Very tight schedule, saith God, and I am not going to be one moment late. I'm going to be right on time

And there are some that continue to want to stand in my way, to resist. Well, I'll just have to set you aside

And move on. But I'm not going to wait any longer. I'm moving by my power and by My Spirit and the

Whole earth will be filled with my glory, 'here I come, saith the Lord. Before the end of this year, before 1996 comes, there will be a hundredfold increase in this area in

The healing power of God, in the miracles of God, in people turning to me that up to now and before now

Prophecies for Canada

1995 Canada Victory Campaign - Kenneth Copeland - Thurs, Oct. 26 7:30

p.m. - cont'd

Had no time for me, and in the _ow of financial blessing and the power of My Spirit to cause people to

Have more than enough to do what I ask them to do? Before 1996 comes. And by the end of the first two weeks of December 1995, many, many, many of you in this building

Tonight will look at your affairs and look at your physical body and look at your finances and look at your

Families and you'll say, "Look, look, look. It's all come to pass. It's all changed. It's all changed. It's all Changed. And it hasn't been but a few weeks. It's all changed."

"Ahhhhhh, but I don't see how He could do it." I didn't say anything about you being able to see it. I

Can, will and fully plan to do exceeding, abundantly beyond all you ask or think. It's already started. It has

Already begun.

So rejoice and doubt not. Stop and do not continue to say, "I don't know how we'll ever get out of

This. I don't know how we can ever succeed; we're so far behind and so deep in debt." Begin to say, "Well, Thank God, I'll stand in the midst of my dream. I'll have my needs met and my debts paid. I will walk free

And I will be able to do those things that I've always wanted to do. I'll be able to give the way I want to give. I'll be able to take care of my family the way I want to. I will be able to."

And you will too, saith the Lord. Now I could tell you some things, saith the Spirit of God, about

1996, but it's so great you wouldn't believe them yet if I did.

Praise the Lord. Let's give the Lord Praise and thanksgiving.

CANADA - GOD'S CHOSEN ANCHOR RUNNER

Over the past few weeks the Lord has been stirring my heart in regard to

Canada's destiny and a coming invasion of the angelic host. God has chosen specific nations, released to run at appointed times in History as the catalyst for the unfolding of His transcendent plan. The primary example being Israel, the nation chosen for the establishment of the Throne of God, the container of the whole counsel of God, and the centre of His administrations through whom He has moved out to take dominion of the earth. From Jerusalem, to Judea, to Samaria the Gospel went to the ends of the earth, by way of certain Gentile nations raised up in appointed seasons. Through Rome, Christianity spread throughout Europe and on to Africa, from Constantinople to the Soviet Union; through Spain to the Americas and through Great Britain to the Commonwealth nations. It is very important to understand that no nation can usurp the position God has ordained for Israel, or represents the

Promised Land from where Jesus will rule and reign over the earth!

The United States of America was held in reserve and honored as a land of promise for the escape of religious persecution and to also take the Gospel to the world. God has given the United States great military power as a force to restrain evil on earth. The United States was also chosen to stand as a strong ally and friend to the nation of Israel, to support its growth, guard His purposes contained in it, and protect it from the enemies of God! The USA has recently been wavering in this God given mandate.

Also held in reserve for such a time, God is now set to bring forth the last catalytic nation to the forefront — Canada. Canada has been chosen to play a significant role in the completion of God's intentions in the last days before His return! Canada's mandate is not in relation to its military might but rather, God will invest this nation with spiritual might and authority to enforce key strategies and divine tactical maneuvers in His end-time campaign.

While writing this word, in reference to Canada, I heard the Lord say, *"Last Runner."* In researching that phrase I discovered that the last runner in a relay race is called the ANCHOR RUNNER. The anchor runner is responsible for **preserving the lead already secured on the anchor leg or last leg of the race!**

God has prepared Canada for the glory of His Presence, as the Anchor Runner in the last leg of the Divine Journey, to lead in the work to prepare the last day sanctuary that receives Christ! Canada will be used by God to bring forth the yet awaited revelation of the One New Man that Jesus died for, in an authentic union with Israel and with God! Canada will become a sign and wonder to the nations as a nation that resides under the Glory, favor and blessing of God by its choice to bless Israel! The three crowns that form the maple leaf on the Canadian flag represent God's call and authority to release His healing to the nations. The two bars of red on either side of the leaf represent the Blood and the double supernatural 'Grace, Grace' to complete the work to bring forth the Headstone — an apostolic generation raised up as the Mature Man, in a Holy union of purpose with Christ! (Zech. 4:7, Eph. 4:13).

The great nation of Canada is poised at

the entrance of a season of great national revival! The Church of Canada must make the choice to AWAKEN AND ARISE, to triumph over the forces of darkness pressing in at its gates, with determination to overtake the nation. It is time for Canada to arise to the Glorious destiny Almighty God has purposed for it! This Mighty move of His Spirit has been revealed to many prophetic voices dating back as far as 1776:

Around 1776 zealous Americans sought to persecute the British Empire Loyalists who had turned north to settle in Canada in order to remain under the British rule. The Spirit of the Lord spoke through the prophets of the Puritan Reformers saying: "Do not hinder these people, let them move to Canada. Do not seek to incorporate the land of Canada into America. I am in the independence of America from Britain, and will mightily use this country. But Canada has been reserved by Me for the last days for a special work." (Peter Marshall: The Light and The Glory)

Canada has been ordained by God FOR A SPECIAL WORK, to play a critical role in the outworking of God's plan to unveil the Bride of Christ in preparation for union with the Bridegroom. This nation has an ambassadorial call, to apostolic leadership, to represent God's strategies for the closing of this age, and for the unification of the Body of Christ, in its transformation into the Bride of Christ! In years past I have had three significant revelations from God in regard to Canada that I believe have been reserved for now.

PROPHETIC PERSPECTIVES

In the first vision I saw the map of North America, and as I looked at the map Canada shifted and was lifted up as a holy offering onto God. As I continued to look, the entire nation burst into fiery red and golden flames. As I continued to marvel at this site the nation was raised upward and became a Golden Crown. I believe Canada is a nation where God will establish His Throne of righteousness and justice!

The second revelation I received came as I was leading an Intercessory prayer meeting for Canada; as we were praying, the Lord led me to Luke 14:7-11 a parable about a wedding feast:

"So He told a parable to those who were invited, when He noted how they chose the best places, saying to them: "When you are invited by anyone to a wedding feast, do not sit down in the best place, lest one more honorable than you be invited by him; and he who invited you and him come and say to you, 'Give place to this man,' and then you begin with shame to take the lowest place. But when you are invited, go and sit down in the lowest place, so that when he who invited you comes he may say to you, 'Friend, go up higher."

The Lord then said that Canada had been faithful over the years to remain in the background in humility, that it was time for Canada to come to the forefront and take its place in the destiny of God, as He intends to show up in this nation in a mighty and momentous move! God is now saying to Canada: "FRIEND, COME UP HIGHER, RECEIVE THE

GLORY OF MY PRESENCE THAT IS COMING UPON YOU."

The third revelation God gave me was through a dream: I was on a white horse seated behind the Lord, holding on to Him. I was wearing a Bridal dress and the train was very long and blowing in the wind as we were flying above the clouds. We then descended through the clouds and I began to see the earth below. We flew closer to the earth towards North America. I then saw Canada. We flew very quickly toward its Eastern coast line then suddenly stopped just outside of Canada.

We sat there looking across the nation of Canada; it was very bright, lit up with *white light*. Wide beams of white light were extending up into the heavens from the entire nation, coast to coast. I then saw a thick white cloud descending over Canada. As I looked closer I then realized that it was not a cloud at all, but rather, thousands and thousands of angels descending upon the nation. We stayed outside of Canada observing this; there was the sense in me, almost of urgency — more like a striving to get moving and enter the nation. I wanted to prompt the horse and move the Lord to enter... the vision then ended.

As I prayed to the Lord about what this meant, and why we did not enter, I sensed that it was *not yet time*! That in the fullness of time HE WOULD ENTER, and when He did enter, all Canada would know it! The white beams of light ascending to Heaven represented the intercessory prayers of the saints that have been going up through a multitude of prayer movements and Houses of Prayer, all across this nation from coast to coast. As a result an invasion of the angelic host was being released to prepare the nation for a mighty end-time move of God!

Numerous nations around the earth such as Korea have heard God's call to prayer for Canada and hundreds of thousands have been faithfully praying over the years! Many prophets and leaders have prophesied great things for Canada such as Yonggi Cho, Kenneth Copeland, Cindy Jacobs and Chuck pierce (*many of these prophecies can be found on the internet*). Leaders such as David Damien — an Egyptian Christian, must be honored for answering the call to come to Canada to lay the groundwork of cleansing the land of antisemitism and prejudice, to prepare it for its Divine historic mandate!

Over history God has used key nations as runners to carry the baton on the Divine journey of the Ascent to Union with Christ! As in a relay race, each runner must hand off the baton to the next runner within the assigned zone. We are now entering the zone of the *Fullness of Times* — the time of completion of the House of God and the summing up of all things in Christ, contained in the dynamics of the Feast of Tabernacles. This will be fulfilled in the season of *Parousia* — the Season of His Presence — the season of the closing of the age, when the level of His Presence will rise exponentially, culminating with His return! It is time to bless Canada, to intercede for Canada, to cheer her on in her call to run the race well, to finish the Divine circuit and hand the baton back to Israel, as the Body — the One New Man, in a unity of purpose, work together to prepare the way for the return of the King of kings!

Now, my son, may the LORD be with you; and may you prosper, and build the house of the LORD your God, as He has said to you. Only may the LORD give you wisdom and understanding, and give you charge concerning Israel, that you may keep the law of the LORD your God… Therefore arise and build the sanctuary of the LORD God, to bring the ark of the covenant of the LORD and the holy articles of God into the house that is to be built for the name of the LORD." 1Chronicles 22:9-14

In long relays, runners begin by jogging while looking back at the incoming runner and holding out a hand to receive the baton. I believe God is saying to America, that *CANADA HAS BEGUN TO RUN*; she has been looking back to you over the years, receiving much treasure from you, and now, is now holding out her hand, to take her place in the race and run the Anchor Leg to the finish line! Canada and the United States share the longest border in the world, we are friends, allies and most importantly we share a divine destiny in Christ to partner together to serve the purposes of the King. I believe God is asking the United States and all nations to now stand with Canada and under-gird His purposes with prayer & intercession!

After reading these prophetic words for Canada a person wants to stand up and rejoice. Problem is though when you look around all you see are churches building their empires with little regard to the kingdom of God. The cessation people are loudly screaming from the pulpit that tongues, prophecy, and the prophet's ministry as well as miracles have all passed away. The cessation doctrine leaves the church powerless and weak. A powerless weak church can't stand against the wiles of the enemy but just rolls over and hopes for some mercy before the enemy destroys them. This is a major deception and those who partake of this false doctrine and will fall into the hand of the enemy.

We can't look at what we see. In times past when it looked like devil is winning God has a remnant of people who stand faithful to His Word, His righteousness, His will and Glory. Are you part of the remnant who will seek God to heal our land and have His dominion flow across our land from sea to sea? The remnant need to be in intercessory prayer for God to heal our land pour out His Spirit and Glory upon us like never in the history of this planet. Then I believe we shall see a great revival in the church and an awakening to God in the world system.

TOMMY HICKS VISION – 1961

"I had hardly fallen asleep when the vision and the revelation that God gave to me came before me. The vision came three times, exactly in detail, the morning of July 25th, 1961. I was so stirred and so moved by the revelation, that this has changed by complete outlook upon the body of Christ, and upon the last – the end-time ministry. The greatest thing that the church of Jesus Christ has ever been given lies straight ahead."

"As the vision appeared to me, after I was asleep, I suddenly found myself in a great distance. Where I was, I do not know, but as I was looking down upon the earth, suddenly the whole world came into view: every nation, every kindred, every tongue came before my sight, from the east and the west, from the north and the south. And I recognized every country and many cities that I had been in. I was almost in fear and trembling as I stood beholding the great sight before me. At that moment, when the world came into view, it began to lightning and thunder. As the lightning flashed over the face of the earth, my eyes went downward – and I was facing north."

"Suddenly I beheld what looked like a great giant; and as I stared and looked at it, I was almost bewildered by the sight. It was so gigantic and was so great in stature; his feet seemed to reach to the north pole and his head to the south; his arms were stretched from sea to sea. I could not even begin to understand whether this was a mountain or whether this be a giant, but as I watched it, I suddenly beheld this great giant. I could see it was struggling for life, to even live. His body was covered with debris from head to foot. At times this great giant would move its body and act as if it would even rise up. When it did, thousands of little creatures seemed to run away – hideous looking creatures would run away from this giant. When he would become calm, they would come back. All of a sudden this great giant lifted his hand toward the heavens, and then it lifted its other hand. When it did, these creatures by the thousands seemed to flee away from this giant and go out into the darkness."

"Slowly this great giant began to rise, and as he did, his head and hands went into the clouds. As he arose to his feet, he seemed to have cleansed himself from the debris and filth that was upon him, and he began to raise his hands into the heavens as though praising the Lord. As he raised his hands it wan even unto the clouds. Suddenly every cloud became silver, the most beautiful silver I have ever known. As I watched the phenomenon, it was so great; I could not even begin to understand what it all meant. I was so stirred as I watched it, and I cried unto the Lord, and said, "Oh Lord, what is the meaning of this?" It felt as if I was actually in the Spirit, and could feel the presence of the Lord even as I was asleep. From those clouds suddenly there came great drops of liquid light raining down upon this mighty giant, and slowly, slowly, this giant began to melt – began to sink, as it were, into the very earth itself. As he melted, his whole form seemed to have melted upon the face of the earth, and this great rain began to come down; liquid drops of light, as it were, began to flood the very earth itself. As I watch this giant that seemed to melt, suddenly it became millions of people over the face of the earth. As I beheld the sight before me, people stood up over the world. They were lifting their hands and they were praising the Lord."

"At that very moment there came a great thunder that seemed to roar from the heavens. I turned my eyes toward the heavens, and suddenly I saw a figure in white, in glistening white – the most glorious thing that I have ever seen in all my life. I did not see the face, but somehow I knew that it was the Lord Jesus Christ. He stretched forth His hand upon the peoples and nations of the world, men and women. As He pointed toward them, this liquid light seemed to flow from His hand into these persons, and a mighty anointing of God came upon them, and those people began to go forth in the name of the Lord. And this is the miracle of it – this is the glorious miracle of it – those people would stretch forth their hands exactly as the Lord did, and it seemed that there was the same liquid fire in their hands. As they stretched forth their hands, they said, "According to my word, be thou made whole." As these people continued in this mighty ministry, I did not fully realize what it was. And I looked to the Lord and said, "What is the meaning of this?" And He said, "This is that that I will do in the last days. I will restore all that the cankerworm, the palmerworm, the caterpillar – I will restore all that they have destroyed. This, My people in the end-time, shall go forth. As a mighty army shall they sweep over the face of the earth."

"One of the things that seemed remarkable – after I had reviewed the vision so many times in my mind – I never saw a church and I never saw or heard anything of a denomination, but these people were going in the Name of the Lord of hosts. Hallelujah! As they marched forward, everything they did was the ministry of Christ. These people were ministering to the multitudes over the face of the earth. Tens of thousands, yea, millions came to the Lord Jesus Christ as these people stood forth and gave the message of the Kingdom – of the coming of the Kingdom – in this hour."

"Suddenly there was another loud clap of thunder that seemed to resound around the world. I heard again the voice, the voice that seemed to speak: "Now, this is My people. This is My beloved bride." When the voice spoke, I looked upon the earth and I could see the lakes and the mountains. The graves were opened and people from all over the world, the saints of all ages, seemed to be rising, and as they rose from the graves, suddenly all these people came from every direction and they seemed to be forming again this gigantic body. I could hardly comprehend it, it was so marvelous – it was so far beyond anything I could ever dream or think of. But, as this body suddenly began to form – it took shape again in the form of this mighty giant – this time it was different. It was arrayed in the most beautiful, gorgeous white – its garments were without spot or wrinkle – as this body began to form. The people of all ages appeared to be gathering into this body. Slowly, slowly, as it formed up into the very heavens, suddenly from the heavens above the Lord Jesus came – became the Head. I heard another clap of thunder that said, "This is My beloved Bride for whom I have waited. She will come forth, even tried by fire. This is she that I have loved from the beginning of time" - end quote.

EPILOGUE

Therefore, as the elect of God, holy and beloved, put on tender mercies, kindness, humility, meekness, longsuffering; bearing with one another, and forgiving one another, if anyone has a complaint against another; even as Christ forgave you, so you also must do. But above all these things put on love, which is the bond of perfection. And let the peace of God rule in your hearts, to which also you were called in one body; and be thankful.
Colossians 3:12-15 NKJV

This book is about preparing you for tomorrow, hopefully directing you to a more serious relationship with Jesus and people around you. When you are

faithful to walk in the fruit of the Spirit
and value all that are within the sphere
of your influence, God will increase
your sphere of influence and show you
and prepare you for the second.

BIO

William carries the anointing of a prophet and psalmist. He is also a Bible teacher, author and international speaker. He operates in all of the Spiritual gifts. He uses the gifts as the Holy Spirit wills. One of William's great desires is to lead others to Christ and to follow Holy Spirit wherever He leads.

www.ingramcontent.com/pod-product-compliance
Lightning Source LLC
Chambersburg PA
CBHW051043030426
42339CB00006B/166